CLASSROOM CLANGERS

CLASSROOM CLANGERS

Selected and compiled by

John G. Muir

Illustrated by GEORGE J. GLASS

GORDON WRIGHT PUBLISHING
25 MAYFIELD ROAD, EDINBURGH EH9 2NQ
SCOTLAND

British Library Cataloguing in Publication Data

Muir, John
   Classroom Clangers.
   1. English wit and humour
   I. Title
   827'.914'08   PN6175

   ISBN 0-903065-49-5

Typeset by Jo Kennedy, Edinburgh
Printed by Billing & Sons Ltd, Worcester

Contents

Preface

When I read *Humour in the Schoolroom*, a collection of pupils'
sayings and writings, by the late Robert Strachan, I was inspired
to update it adding some from my own experience as a teacher. I
am grateful to his family for allowing me to use some of the
material from his book. I trust they will see *Classroom Clangers*
as a dedication to him as well as to other colleagues in the
teaching profession who have managed to survive daily between
nine and four because of their quick wit and sense of humour.

John G. Muir

A Teacher's Lot

A headmaster wrote in a book many years ago, 'Teachers are gradually moving towards a place in the sun more commensurate with the value of their services to the State. Popular opinion, however, still seems to err about the nature of their work.' viz:

Teaching always drives a man to drink, golf, or insanity.

Teaching is for men that cannot find labouring jobs to suit their state of health.

A teacher is a cross between a nurse and a policeman.

If she doesn't get married she'll have to stay in teaching all her life.

Poor man, even when he gets married he has to stick at that job.

My daddy's not a gentleman, he's a teacher.

If he has the grace of God we'll put him into the ministry, if not he can go on and become a teacher.

She's just a young lassie but she'll probably be all right if she stays an infant teacher.

You should take up teaching; it's a nice easy job and grand holidays.

She's only got an infant class just now, but if she does well they'll probably put her further up.

He's not really a teacher, he takes P.E.

Dear Teacher

The average parent is an adept apologist as these extracts from notes indicate:

Please excuse Jane for being absent from school. She had an ulster in her throat.

Please excuse Mary for being absent. She will be absent a long time. The doctor says she has an absent in the brain.

Jessie cannot come to school as she has haricot veins.

Please excuse Jenny's absence. She came home on Tuesday afternoon with it and we just can't get rid of it.

Please excuse Moira for not being at school this week. I have been upside down with the painters for the last three days.

John has been in bed for two days with his head.

Although Susan left in good time she had to come back home with her stomach.

I kept Jean at home yesterday because my wife had twins but I can assure you that this will not happen again.

Dear Sir, Tommy is absent because of his face, he has had it a long time and the doctor says it is spreading.

Please excuse Jacqueline for being off school yesterday. She was hanging on to the mantlepiece with her stomach.

Jamie did not attend school yesterday because he was evaporated with constipation.

Lizzie was very bad with pans in her tummy.

Please excuse Mary from being absent but she was kept at home to help her mother wash yours truly her father.

I have been in bed for three days with the doctor and couldn't get up to get him dressed.

I must ask you never to use corpal punishment on Tommy. We never do ourselves except in self-defence.

Dear Sir, thanks for all you have done for our James. May God guard and keep you from Mrs Brown.

Although she has been learning shorthand for a year at your school she cannot speak it yet.

Sorry John is off but he has information of the lungs, with combinations.

Dear Sir, please excuse Sebastian for being absent from school as he had Diahero.

Sometimes the pupils' excuses are equally amusing:

Please sir my mother was making jam and I had to go to the cemetry for jars.

I was off because my mother went to hospital to get me a wee brother. I'm back because it's a sister I've got and my father's got my auntie to live with us just now. He's going to try and get me a wee brother.

I went home to find out what time it was, that's why I was late, sir.

I thought the clock had just struck nine sir but it was the half hour.

Please sir it wasn't me, Tommy did it with me.

The Early Years

It was the five-year-old's first day at school and when he was introduced to the infant teacher she showed him to his seat in the classroom. He never said a word throughout the whole morning session but the patient teacher did not force him to join in with the others but left him to his own devices amongst the toys, assuming he would come round. He looked around the toys, equipment and pictures while the teacher talked to groups of children. Only occasionally, when she gently scolded a child, did the little fellow raise his head, look at her and frown. Towards the end of the day, when she hoped he would have settled down, she was pleased to see him approaching her desk to say something. He shocked the prim infant teacher with, 'This is a hell of a place this, I'm going home, and I'll not be back.'

The tall, bald-headed headmaster was trying to impose his presence on a rather noisy group of first day pupils in the dining room. They weren't sure who he was and he wasn't making much of an impression on them. Standing in the middle of the dining room, and at the point of raising his voice, he was aware of a tug on his trouser leg. Looking down, he saw a little fellow with custard on his jersey beaming into his face. 'Hey mister, you look like Kojak.'

The infant teacher had the new entrants line up to go on their first visit to the gym. Setting off along the corridor, she was aware that a little boy had started to whistle merrily. When she asked him to stop, he asked 'Why?' 'Well Paul,' she said, just think if I had to allow everyone to whistle along the corridor, what a noise there would be.' Whereupon he retorted, 'Well miss, don't let the rest of them whistle while I'm whistling.'

On her second day at school a little girl was standing quietly at the front of the school long after all the pupils had gone home. Thinking she was looking for her mother the janitor spoke to her. He was amused when she replied, 'No, I always go home myself, but I'm just looking to see where my teacher goes at night.'

13

The class teacher was very interested to notice that the seven-year-old had cut out the multiplication tables from an old jotter and pasted them on to her own. However, when she enquired as to why she had only taken up to the five times table, the little girl boldly replied, 'Well, miss, I'll do these before I leave this school and I'll do the rest when I go to University.'

The teacher had repeatedly checked the girl in her class of five-year-olds for chattering while she was talking to the group. When she started whispering and giggling again she made her stand up and tell the whole class what she was whispering about. Reddening a little the lass, amidst giggles, said, 'I was only telling Susan that I thought you were awful fat.'

A small boy sent to the headmaster for swearing refused to tell the man what he had said and why. Anxious to find out the gravity of the offence, he insisted that the boy tell him and the little lad exclaimed, 'But, sir, I can't say it in front of you,' then added quietly, seeing that the headmaster was still angry, 'but if you tell me a few swear words yourself, I'll tell you when you come to it.'

A pupil, observed fidgeting during a lesson, was taken to task by the teacher, who enquired what he was playing with. The boy went red but made no reply. 'Please miss it's a pin he's got,' a little girl piped up and the offending article was taken away by the teacher from the boy's hand. Later on, when the teacher asked the boy to stand up and read, he reddened again and looked a little frightened. He was normally keen to read out, so she asked him what the matter was. 'Well miss, that pin you took keeps my trousers up.'

A small boy was asked to paint a radiator for a class frieze. (The other children were painting other classroom objects). The teacher found his paper untouched, but the class radiator was a lovely green colour!

Passing the Forestry Building in Edinburgh, which has a lot of smoked glass, the little boy of five asked 'Is that a night school?'

The harassed infant mistress, flinging open the door of the infants' toilet, announced 'Now I'm coming to smack the next bottom that makes a noise in here!'

A little girl was asked why her sister didn't come home with her on the school bus. 'She'll be a long time and won't be home for ages yet,' was the reply. 'Why not?' asked her mother. 'Well, she has been picked as extra prostitute for the netball team because there's one short,' was the answer.

One day the headmaster came into the room and, as he always did, looked at the day's numbers and said, 'Thirty-six present in the morning, only thirty-five in the afternoon, stand up the one who's absent.'

A little girl was asked by her teacher where the dot was that should have gone over the 'i' in her composition. The girl said, 'Oh that's still in the pencil.'

'I hope you will all have a good holiday now boys and girls and come back with some sense in your heads,' the teacher said as the class stood ready to go. 'Same to you, miss,' they replied in unison.

On one occasion a teacher giving a lesson on manners asked, 'Now why do you think a gentleman should always walk on the outside of the pavement when going out with a lady?' There was a dearth of ideas among the class until eventually an enlightening answer was received, 'Please miss, so's he can spit in the gutter?'

An elderly man passing a school playground took a boy to task for being cheeky to him and said, 'You deserve a good thrashing. I wish I was your father.' 'You can if you like,' came the reply, 'My mother's a widow.'

The little girl ran home as fast as she could after her first day at school. 'I'm the prettiest girl in the class Mummy.' 'Who told you that?' the mother asked, laughing. 'Well,' she replied, 'I was there; I saw the others.'

'Well, what did you learn at school today?' the young mother asked her son after his first day at school. 'Nuffing,' came back the reply, 'I've got to go back tomorrow.'

Showing his spots to his classmates, the child, who had clearly contracted the measles, was told by his apparently envious friends, 'Lucky you, tell the teacher and you'll get sent home.' 'No fear,' came back the reply, 'I'll wait till you catch it and then I'll have someone to play with.'

There were hisses from the class when one of their mates presented the teacher with a lovely bunch of flowers. 'How dare you make fun of John for being so kind,' scolded the teacher, 'You must have a lovely garden, John.' 'No miss,' came the quick reply, 'We haven't got a garden, but I do a milk round in the morning.'

In the days when it was normal for young lads to show deference to their elders in the street by lifting their cap, for example, an elderly gentleman complained to the headmaster that a group of boys had been rude to him and walked past him on the pavement without acknowledging his presence. Anxious that the school should keep its good name the headteacher and the staff impressed upon the children the importance of good manners and referred to Mr Tom Glen's visit. Later, meeting the said gentleman at a gate, one of the pupils doffed his cap and held the gate open for him. Very impressed, he gave the lad a coin, saying, 'Someone has taught you manners my boy.' 'Well, sir,' the boy replied, 'I'd get a row from my teacher if I didn't because she said that if ever we saw old Tommy Glen we had to be polite or he'd be up complainin' again.'

The pupil was clearly ashamed to admit that his father was an undertaker when asked about his parent's profession. He neatly evaded the awkward question with, 'Please Sir, he follows the medical profession.'

'My Grandpa has bald hair.'

'Daniel, do you need the toilet?' 'No miss, I'm only warming my feet.'

'What do tigers eat?' 'Frosties.'

'What is the desert full of, Tom?' 'Camels?'

'Is there a special time when you eat turkey?' 'Yes miss, when it's dead.'

A cemetery is where dead people live.

17

Mind Your Language

Here are some short extracts from jotters and exam papers:

People who work for the government are called senile servants.

Barbarians are things put on wheels to make them run smoothly.

A navigator is the strap which a navvy wears under his knees to stop rats running up his leg.

A buttress is the wife of a butler.

When the airman came to the edge of the volcano he could see the creator smoking.

The appendix is part of a book for which no one has yet discovered a use.

Chequers is a public house belonging to the Prime Minister.

A soviet is a cloth used by waiters in hotels.

A welsher is a native of Wales.

To scotch something is to drown your sorrows in whisky.

A mosquito is the child of black and white parents.

Transparent is something you can see through. For example – a keyhole.

Acrimony is another name for marriage.

Polygamy is a shape with many sides to it.

A pagoda is a chair on wheels used for carrying people about.

To be 'called to the Bar' is to be treated to a drink.

'Unaware' means your vest and pants.

The Last Post is always sounded by a lone burglar.

'Now children,' said the teacher, 'I want you to write me a story. Something different. Something you haven't thought of before. Write what is inside you at this very moment.' One of the stories ran: 'Inside of me there is my heart, my liver, lots of other parts and of course the mince and stewed prunes I had for dinner.'

'The cat is a quadruped, the legs as usual being at the four corners. Do not tease cats, because firstly, it is wrong to do so and secondly, because of his clawses which is longer than people think. Cats have nine lives, but it is seldom required in this country because of Christianity.'

'Where would you put the colon?' 'On the fire, sir.'

A kite is a light wooden frame covered with paper and is sent into the air by boys with tails on them.

Everyone staying in the house on the day of the census must be filled in or else.

A brewery is a place where beer is buried.

The man found hanging outside the bank was acting in a peculiar way.

My mum uses polythene for my dad's food.

People go self cantering at Butlin's Holiday Camp.

We have got a new home copulator.

The sponsored walk was organised by the school to help cripple children.

Orange juice must be deluded.

A man with a wife and two children got about five times as much as a man not married with no children so men were desperately trying to get married and to get lots of children.

In 19th century Britain because of the squalor, people found they were going back instead of forward.

The company turned into a liquid to pay off its debts.

When the X-ray van came we had to take off some of our clothes in a cuticle.

'What is the plural of potato?' 'Turnip, sir?'

They are putting up a new building in town for the farewell officers.

I like Mrs McKinnon, she gives us pea tea.

A deacon is something you put on a hill and set fire to it.

'Give a sentence including "human race".' 'My dad ran in the human race.'

I had to consume the rubber before I was awarded a new one.

I felt sacred as I walked to the dentist's.

The indication for right is to put your hand out a few yards, before turning off.

A cloister is when things are bundled up together.

Luxury means when you like it and cuddle down to it.

Massacre is black stuff people put on their eyes.

Amphibious – a Greek God.

Pluto took Persephone on the Underground.

d.c. = dead.

Why are there inverted commas around 'patient'?
So that the blood will flow easily into the bottle placed tactfully under the bed.

A Black Maria is a person who needs blood urgently or she will die.

A white collar worker is a lavadry cleaner.

A young horse is called a clot.

(From a letter of application). Perhaps you would like to see me in your convenience.

Aquamarine – a soldier specialising in underwater swimming.

A deaf mute is a deaf dog.

Inspired means they had it coming to them.

Q. Give the masculine equivalent of the following: Filly.
A. Empty.

Soldiers the next in rank below sargeants are called corpusles.

The men of the little fishing village used their wives to bait their lines. Although it was sore they did not mind. Sometimes however they mended their nuts.

When my grandfather died he had a mementary put up at the end of his grave.

I must draw a one-inch virgin on the left hand side of each page.

Plumb – a thing that cleans drains out.
       – fattish.

Immobile – mobile means to make smaller e.g. a mobile library, so immobile means to make larger.

Neap – A drink without water in it.
      – A pile of something.
      – Tidy.
      – Large.

Palpable – squashable – to mash.

Silhouette – to turn round on the spot.

Hamlet – a little eggs beaten up with some bacon.

A paltry attempt – a place where you try to keep hens.

They had 325 guests and relations for dinner at the reception.

Illustrate the difference between two, to and too.
There are two o's in too but only one in two and to.

A costume is so called because it is very expensive.

Another type of wood is hogmanay.

A rudder is used for milking cows.

Monogamy is a kind of furniture.

'What does "saddest" mean?' 'Wood after it has been sad.'

'What do you call someone who sells eggs, butter and cheese?' 'A Pakistani!'

Proverbs:
One swallow doesn't make a dram.
Never look a gift horse up the nose.
Fine feathers make fine cushions.

A watershed is where they keep barges on canals.

During a spelling lesson the teacher wrote the words 'widow' and 'window' on the board. 'Now children,' she said, 'I want you to notice the difference between 'widow' and 'window'. What is it?' 'Please, miss,' was the answer, 'We can see through a window, but we can't see through a widow.'

In the older days they danced round the maypole in May, especially on Mayday. They do not do it now because they call it Labour.

Mayday used to be celebrated by Labour, now it is used by airmen and sailors when they want help.

In spring our local farmer spreads new seeds to feed the crows.

The bride wore orange blossom as a symbol of innocence, purity and future abundance.

When my feet are wet I take them off and dry them at the fire.

A cuckoo is a bird which lays other birds' eggs in its own nest.

When coal runs out we will have to use our brains for fuel.

Spelling errors are often unconsciously humorous:

Some instruments are: viles, cellars, trumpets, hornets, baboons, old boys and bubble bases.

In Spring the woods are beautiful with wild hyacinths and wooden enemies.

My Daddy is a shosho worker (social worker).

A ruminating animal is one which chews its cubs.

Rapids are animals with long ears and nearly no tails.

A mandoline was a high official in China.

At the end of the long race the horse dropped with fatigue and the poor rider was pitched into maternity.

During the war we needed to increase our supplies so the public parks were turned into elopments.

The king wore a scarlet robe trimmed with vermin.

The plural of ox is oxo. The plural of forget-me-not is forget-us-not.

A relative pronoun is a family pronoun such as 'mother', 'brother' and 'aunt'.

A rhinoceros is so called because rind means skin and nocerous nose.

Contralto is a low form of music which only women sing.

A primate is the wife of a premier.

She scar guest dan is the president of France.

The Bible Tells Me So

The teacher was telling the infant class about the birth of Jesus and had reached the point when the wise men appeared to visit the new born Baby. 'And what do you think Mary would have said to the men?' she asked the class. One little voice piped up, 'My Mummy would have said, "What time of night is this to visit a baby?"'

A mother noticed that her child was practising writing the letter 'I' at home and she paused between each letter in the row. Curious, she asked the child what she was doing. The little girl replied, 'Well, the teacher read from the Bible today and said that God said, "Draw an I unto me and I will draw an I unto you."'

When saying his prayers at night the boy was heard to say, 'Please God make Paris the capital of Turkey.' When he repeated it several times he was asked by his mother why such a thing was so important. He replied, 'Because that's what I wrote in my Geography exam.'

In reply to a question on the Ten Commandments, 'Was it lawful to buy or sell on the Sabbath Day?' One child replied, 'Buy'.

When the minister visited the school he spoke to a quiet little lad at the front but could get nothing out of him. He was unaware that he was new to the class that morning. Later he tried to ask him a few questions to involve him. 'Tell me son, what do you know about Jesus?' When he got no reply, the boy next to him piped up, 'Please minister, he doesn't know anything about Jesus, he only came from Glasgow yesterday.'

When R.E. exams came round, some children clearly got several facts mixed up. When asked about animals in the Bible, playing an important part in the life of God's servants, one pupil referred to Balaam's ass who rebuked the man and later on referred to the whale which swallowed Jonah, saying to him, 'Almost thou persuadest me to be a Christian.'

Having explained the meaning of BC to her class, the teacher asked for suggestions as to the meaning of AD, and she got the reply, 'After the Devil'.

The teacher was involved in explaining about angels and seraphs when one child asked if they flew. 'Yes,' said the teacher, 'it says so in the Bible.' 'I'd like to be one,' said one scruffy little lad who was always in trouble. 'That would be nice,' she smiled. '. . . and I could chase the crows, miss,' he continued.

The teacher was fascinated by the pupil's drawing of the Christmas Story. She had drawn a lot of people and a baby in an aeroplane! 'Please miss, that's the flight into Egypt and Pontius the Pilot.'

This was written in an R.E. exam: 'Christ cured Peter's wife's mother, when she was sick of a fever, and Peter cursed and swore and went out and wept bitterly.'

Here are some miscellaneous statements, mostly from written work:

A Job's comforter is a thing you give a baby to give him the patience of Job.

A worshipper of Mammon is a bigamist.

Eastern shepherds were called Easter shepherds because they were on the hills at Easter and they let their sheep gaze in the fields.

The Canaanites were chapel and the Israelites were church.

My uncle Hugh is a Geneva's Witness. He goes to church twice on a Sunday.

As this was a holy day, the priest washed the beggars' feet and gave arms to the poor.

The Muslin faith was started by Mohammed Ali.

A miracle is something that happens unexpectedly like Jairus's daughter.

Jeremiah gave his people a massage.

At Whitsun God gave his disciples the gift of the Holy Goat.

Paraphrase the following: 'God so loved the world . . . that whosoever believeth in him should not perish . . .'
   This means that all who believe in God's son would not freeze but have a long life.

A class was asked to recite the Creed. One boy stood up and said, 'I believe in God Almighty'. Then the teacher asked another boy to say his bit. He stood up and said, 'I believe in Jesus Christ our Lord'. Then there was a silence. Suddenly a boy at the back said, 'Please sir, the boy who believes in the Holy Spirit is off today.'

On the Day of Penticost they all had a touch of the wind.

The first book of the Bible is called Guinness.

Our Father, who art in Heaven,
Harold be Thy name.

The other night I saw some men in town trying to join all the churches together.

The shepherds washed their socks by night.

'Follow me and I will make you vicious old men.'

'Surely good Mrs Murphy shall follow me all the days of my life.'

Lead us not into Drem Station.

29

Medieval Church Law stated that an Authorised Virgin should be chained to every pulpit for the sole use of the clergy.

Thou shalt not admit adultery.

Christians are only allowed one wife. This is called monotony.

Guinnessis is the first book of the Bible, Revolutions is the last.

David killed Goliath with the Axe of the Apostles.

Ambiguity is telling the truth when you don't want to.

Liberty of conscience is doing wrong and not worrying about it afterwards.

An unclean spirit is another name for a dirty devil.

Lot's wife looked round and turned a somersault.

People who are not Jews are called reptiles.

Jesus said that we should lay up trousers in heaven for ourselves.

At the end of the church service the child remarked that they 'had sung the dogs holiday and come home.'

Joseph's family flew into Egypt because there was a feminine in their own land.

A graven image in the Bible is an idle maid with hands.

I don't believe in the Devil. It's like Santa Claus, it's your dad all the time.

Someone who does not believe in God is called a Non-Conformist.

In a Free Church they read from a book called *The Beverages*.

At the Passover the Jews ate level bread.

Hereward was King of the Jews.
Henry Wood was the King of Israel.

King Organstine was the Jewish King.

Paul wrote the Epistle to the Chrysantheans.

The widow's mite was a wee girl healed by Jesus.

Esau was a hairy man in the Bible who wrote fables and sold his copyright for a mess of potash.

What is the chief end of man? His feet.

The teacher was telling her class the Nativity story and was illustrating it with a picture of Mary, Joseph, the Baby Jesus in the manger, flanked by the wise men and the shepherds. She pointed out that poor Mary and Joseph had to spend the night in a stable when Jesus was born. A wee lad piped up: 'Please Miss, they weren't so poor when they got their photos taken!'

When Jesus said, 'No man can have two masters', he meant that a man should only have one wife.

Moses sent ten plagues to Egypt, the last of them, and the worst, was children.

I like the story about the wee boy who stole the priest's watch. (From the hymn, 'The old man meek and mild, the priest of Israel slept: his watch, the temple child, the little Levite kept').

31

The Facts of Life

We live in a day when sex education at school and at home is said to be more prevalent. What do you think?

Twins are two children with the same hair and the same clothes.

Dad wanted to break the news of the addition to the family to his ten-year-old daughter but did not get around to saying anything until the child was born. 'Diane, the fairies have just brought you a baby brother.' 'Lovely,' the girl replied excitedly, 'I must write to John.' Her father was curious to know what she had written to her elder brother who was away from home so he peeped at the letter when she was out. 'Dear John, I told you they had done it. It's come off at last and it's a boy . . . You win!'

Twins are two things which come unexpectedly together.

'Mummy, where did I come from?' the little girl asked one day on returning home from school. Taking this as a golden opportunity the young mother proceeded to explain the facts of life to her daughter. After some time, and some strange faces from the little girl, she piped up. 'Thanks Mummy, I wanted to know because there's a new girl in our class and she says that she comes from Edinburgh.'

Written in a News Book: 'We were going to have a baby some time but not now. Daddy told me where it is and Mummy has swallowed it.'

Boys and girls develop in different places.

It is difficult to tell the sex of my rabbits, but they know, because Billy and Sammy had little ones last week.

'I know where babies come from, Miss, but if I told you, you wouldn't believe me.'

The teacher had been pregnant for some time but none of the pupils in her infant class seemed to have noticed her steady growth until one day the dental hygienist called to talk to them about teeth and explained that sweets and chocolates were not only bad for teeth but made you fat, if you ate too many. On returning to the classroom one little lad walked up to the teacher and said, pointing to her tummy, 'I know what you've been doing miss!'

Know Your Authors

Shakespeare:

Shakespeare was a very polite man. He often said 'Go to . . .' but never finished the sentence.

Most of Shakespeare's plays are terrible tragedies.

Shakespeare made a mistake in mentioning Galen, who did not live till a hundred years after his time.

In Shakespeare's play Omlet, we read that . . .

One of Shakespeare's plays was called Charlie's Aunt.

The chief feature of the play *Richard II* is the decomposition of the king.

Jonson, Milton, Chaucer *et al.*

Milton was made Poet Orient.

Chaucer lived in London. He translated the Bible, and was put in jail.
    After doing nothing for some time, he came to the conclusion that he might as well write another book, and then wrote the *Pilgrim's Progress*.

Bunyan was the inventor of the Nonconformost Religion and also wrote the *Pilgrim's Progress*.

In 1620 the Pilgrim Fathers crossed the ocean. This was called the Pilgrim's Progress.

Pope wrote chiefly in cutlets.

Tennyson wrote a book called In Memorandum.

Sir Walter Scott was known as the Blizzard of the North. He failed in his attempt to reach the North Pole.

Socrates died from an overdose of wedlock.

When Caesar died he said, 'Ate two Brutes'.

If it had not been for the love of liquor Burns might have been with us yet.

After twice committing suicide, Cowper lived till 1800 when he died a natural death.

Charles Lamb is my favourite author. He had touches of insanity.

My favourite poem is Garve's Elegy.

Hopefully Historical

The teacher warned the class not to spend a lot of time writing about Alfred burning the cakes in the swineherd's house but to tell of his work for the people and welfare of his country. When the exam came along one girl wrote: 'Alfred, among other things which he did, paid a visit to the cottage of a swineherd's wife but the less that is said about this the better.'

Julius Caesar landed in Britain in 55 BC and went away in AD 410.

In 1314 King Robert the Bruce won the Bannock of Battleburn.

Lord Nelson's last words at the Battle of Trafalgar as he waved his arms over the noise was, 'Peace be still'. When he had finished his last words he plunged his head into Captain Hardy's chest and all was over.

The Battle of Trafalgar Square was fought in London against the Spaniards.

Mary Queen of Scots had no time to say her last words for her head came off too suddent.

History tells us that Oliver Cromwell was afraid of nothing except his wife.

During the Black Hole of Calcutta one hundred and forty-six men were confined all night in a cellar with one widow and in the morning only twenty three staggered forth alive and they were romantic with thirst.

Clive imprisoned 146 men in the Black Hole of Calcutta and so laid the foundations for the British Empire.

Charles II told the people that they could now do as they

pleased, get drunk or gamble. This was called the Restoration.

The Great Fire of London was caused by someone dropping a match into a tin of petrol in a garage.

Mary Queen of Scots was beheaded for her part in the Badminton Plot.

Mary Queen of Scots married the Dolphin of France.

The Young Pretender was quite harmless, as was seen by the way he was hidden by the maid in Scotland.

The King of Spain was very angry when Columbus discovered America, but it wasn't Columbusses' fault. He didn't look for it, because he never new it was there. His boat just dunted into it.

Henry the Eighth was said to iron his trousers on his wife's back. (From 'meanwhile, Henry was pressing his suit on Anne Boleyn'!)

Who invented gunpowder? A lady who wanted guns to look nice.

The Highland Clearances was a big sale of sheep in the North of Scotland.

King William had a new forrest maid and he killed everyone who chased his dear.

Nelson had a column put up for him in Trafalgar Square. It is high so that everyone can see where he fell and remember him for his extinguished conduct for England.

James the First claimed the throne of England through his mother as he had no father to speak of.

Victoria was the longest queen that ever ruled in Britain. She was a good woman but I don't think she ever married. Her daughter was Queen Elizabeth.

At the Battle of Hastings William ordered his archers to shoot at the thickest part of the English so they shot upwards so that the arrows might fall on their heads.

During King John's reign England was placed under an interdict and the Pope stopped all births, marriages and deaths for a year.

The Magna Carta said that the King could not order taxis without the consent of parliament.

The Duke of Wellington had a splendid funeral. It took twelve men to carry the beer.

The Ministry of Defence provides clergymen to speak to soldiers.

Revolution is the kind of government they have abroad.

The King's Pardon was what a woman got when she had triplets.

Columbus circumcised the world with a 40ft clipper. The church was against such things but the king of his country was all for it as it brought them fame and money.

Another name for the German Emperor was 'the Geyser'.

During the American Wars of Independence, Lord North-cliffe wisely gave the Irish Volunteers Home Rule.

The Salic Rule said that no man born of woman could obtain the French crown.

After Culloden Prince Charlie roamed around the moors disguised as a pheasant.

Lord Lister invented plasteur of Paris for the cure of sceptic diseases.

The inflammability of the Pope was proclaimed in the Vatican Degrees.

The Pope lives in the Vacuum.

39

The Peninsular War started when John Wesley invaded Portugal.

The Glorious First of June was fought on June 1st.

Everybody was killed at the Battle of Edgehill but they all carried on fighting, and the cavalry advanced backwards.

The Romans came to Britain because there was no room at Rome.

Julius Caesar was a Greek ruler. He was Emperor. He must of been bonkers to burn down Rome, but when he was assassinated he could do nothing more.

General Custer was the leader of the Roundheads.

Habeus Corpus was a man who died in battle.

Elizabethan men wore pointed goblets.

The Puritans did not like the Bishops to wear any clothing.

From a History exam paper:
   Q. What is a mummy?
   A. A body raped in fine linen, and reserved.
   Q. When were the Middle Ages?
   A. 40 to 50.

What was the Roman Forum? Something they sat on.

What was done by coopers? They sold groceries.

King Richard led a crusade to the Holy Land to fight the Saccharins.

The Plimsoll Line was introduced so that sheep wouldn't sink.

40

Queen Elizabeth rode through Coventry with nothing on and Sir Walter Raleigh offered her his cloak. She later had him beheaded.

Mary Queen of Scots lost the Bottle of Langsyne near Glasgow in 1568.

The Bloody Statute was another name for Queen Mary. She was called this because she wouldn't talk.

The housewives of Paris sat and knitted while the guillemot did its deadly work.

Muskets were so heavy that musketeers would have a rest.

Some Puritans had three ears cut off.

You always knew if you had the plague because you died.

As the Spanish Fleet sailed into the English Channel, Drake said, 'The Armada can wait, my bowels can't.'

In Normandy they had Gateaux which were like castles and mansions put together.

One of the tribes of South Africa are called Hotipots.

Q. How did you know if you had the plague?
A. There was a red cross on the door.

The 14th July in France is the Baskabill's Day.

The Mayflower was the ship that was used to find the treasure in *Treasure Island.*

A great Elizabethan sailor who sailed round the world was Charles Drake.

The tomb of Totem Carmen was opened in Egypt.

41

At the end of the year Mr. Macmillan planed to reshape his cabinet.

The inhabitants of South America were Inkers.

The Japanese over-ran China and even occupied Formica.

Queen Victoria's husband was King Victoria.

Disraeli was a man of principle; he married a rich woman for her money.

Karl Marx was one of the famous Marx Brothers. He founded the International Working Mens Federation and had the misfortune to invent Communism.

Charles Colling bred Durham shorthorn cows with his brother Robert.

The Battle of Hastings was between William the Concera and Saladin. It was fort on Mount Carmel.

The Ancient Britons ploughed their fields with elephants.

Napoleon complained that his soldiers marched on his belly.

The Luddites were given a capital punishment – namely death.

Palestine was important because it layed on a camel root.

The Pilgrim Fathers did not find it easy to found a Colony as so many had been found already.

The Protestants disliked the smell of the incest in the Catholic Church.

The King sold foreign policies to make money.

Martin Luther was famous for his Diet of Worms. He said, 'Heaven help me I can take no other course,'

John Knox was born in Haddington, Scotland, little thinking he would become a great reformer.

Van Goch committed suicide by cutting off his ear.

'Habeus corpus' means 'you may have the body'. This was during the Great Plague.

Marat was stabbed by a lady in his bath.

The Bastile was stormed by a number of people called Parisites.

Wellington's nickname was Ironpants.

William the Conqueror spent a phew nights in Canterbury.

Most Norman architecture was built in the olden days.

The first man to sail around the world was Milligan.

Henry II never wore clothes except when he was hawking.

Henry II was an ill-manured man.

The first British Martyr was Harold Wilson.

The Spinning Jenny was worked by a cock which you knocked from one side of the machine to the other.

Victorian ladies had thrills around their bottoms.

The Beefeaters had weapons twenty feet long.

The Puritans sometimes wore a white collar, but that was all.

Henry VIII quarrelled with the Pope because he marred his brother's wife.

In Tudor times women had square chests.

The return of Charles II to the throne was called the Resurrection.

Mungo Park led some kind of exhibition somewhere. He stopped a war or something.

Pompeii was destroyed in a night by an overflow of saliva.

Joan of Arc was burned to a steak for her good deeds.

In the political world today we are faced with the choice of Free Trade or Detection.

The Court of the Chancery is so called because there is not a chance that you will get your money back, when it has once been looked after by it.

George Washington was famous for wasting his father's plum tree and saying, 'Yes, I done it; I cannot tell a lie; thank God I have done my duty.'

The Root and Branch Bill ordered farmers to prune their trees every year.

The Peasants Revolt was caused by placing a poultice (poll tax) on the head of every person over sixteen.

For services rendered at Locarno, Sir Austen Chamberlain was knighted and his wife damed.

The Great Fire of London really did a great deal of good. It purged the city from the plague and burned down eighty-nine churches.

The Black Prince died of injuries received by his horse.

Napoleon's aim was to capture the sea.

The Romans built Hadrian's Wall so they could jump over it and surprise the Scots.

The Navigation Act prohibited any goods from being exported except to the country where they were manufactured.

Triangles and Test Tubes

Geometry teaches us to bisect angels.

A theorum – derived from theos a god and res a thing – is a problem demanding divine intelligence.

Algebraic symbols are used when you don't know what you are talking about.

Geometry teaches us to prove what we already know to be true.

Things which are halves of themselves are equal to each other.

A solid is that which has no space under the circumference.

Parallel lines, even if produced to eternity, cannot expect to meet unless you bend them.

If two triangles have two sides of the one equal to three angles of the other, each to each, to which the opposite sides are also equal, the triangles shall be equal in all respects.

The line opposite the right angle is called the hippotamus.

The hypoteneuse is the line which when someone saw when he was having a bath he shouted, 'I've found it!' and ran out naked to tell everyone.

A circle is a round straight line with a hole in the middle.

Q: The electrolyte used in the manufacture of aluminium has a very high melting point. How is this lowered?
A: Using a crane.

Sir Isaac Newton invented gravity when an apple fell on his head.

Digestion is brought on by the lungs having something the matter with them.

We should all chew well because it is important that we should domesticate our food.

The blood consists of red and white corkscrews.

If you did not eat for sixty days you would die within a month.

An average is something that hens lay on.

The best way to keep milk from going sour is to keep it in the cow.

A fatal disease is the worst type you can have.

If you place a person who has fainted in a lying posture and keep him quiet he will come round.

Water is composed of two gins; oxygin and hydrogin.

X rays are produced when the sun's rays cross each other.

Because hot air rises it is warmer at the top of a mountain.

The weather at the North Pole is so bad that the towns there are not inhabited.

The effect of lead in water is that it sinks in it.

Teacher to pupils: 'This is an axle in my hand. At the end of this axle is a crank.
Pupil: 'Which end, sir?'

Hire purchase are things you can buy in most shops.

To remove air from a flask, pour the water out and put the cork in quick.

A magnetic force is a straight line, generally a curved one, which would tend to point to where the North Pole comes.

Mechanically a long pump handle is better because you can get someone to help you.

Ammonium chloride is also called silly maniac.

Through experiment we soon became the masters of steam and eccentricity.

Geographically Speaking

The whole world lies in a temperence zone except the United States.

Britain has a temporary climate.

The tropic of Cancer is a strange incurable disease.

In the Highlands distilling is the only industry carried to excess.

Crewe is the biggest conjunction in England.

The sun never sets on the British Empire because the Empire was on the East and the sun always sets on the West.

In India the people are divided into castes and outcasts.

The tributaries of the Nile are called Juveniles.

The World makes a resolution every 24 hours.

In Russia there are vast carnivorous forests.

Cologne is famous for the odour made there.

The Seaports of Russia are too far inland for trading purposes.

In the United States people are put to death by elocution.

A mountain range was a cooking stove used at high altitudes.

The population was very dense because of the smoke coming from the chimneys.

Cyclones are the evaporation of volcanoes.

Equinoxes are people who live in igloos in Greenland.

Herrings go about the sea in shawls.

Volcanoes are due to the infernal heat of the earth.

A blizzard is the inside of a hen.

'Name the five continents.' 'a, e, i, o, u.'

The Red Sea is joined to the Mediterranean by the Sewage Canal.

Chicago is a large town at the bottom of Lake Michigan.

The Hindus and Muslims are very religious people. They will have nothing to do with each other.

For most of the year the rivers of Queensland are mere poodles.

My uncle lives in the knighted steaks of America.

A cannibal is two men who kill one another.

A dingo is a bird with the face of a dog.

All French men are alcoholics because they do not drink orange juice and tea like we do.

There is a saying – 'The Englishman eats to live, the Frenchman eats to die'.

The French built the Sacre Coeur Church in memory of a plague sent by the Germans.

You can buy coffee or a bear in French cafes.

My Auntie Jenny went on holiday to Venice and had a great time on a gondolier.

Where are the Urals? Behind the Science lab, sir.

French cooks spend a long time papering food.

In France the meal at 4.30 p.m. is bread and pain.

The oldest member of the Commonwealth is 108.

The Zulus live in mud huts and have rough mating on the floor.

A lumberjack is what you cut down trees with.

Latitude tells us how far we are North or South of a Quaker.

Transhumance is changing men into elephants.

The savage which is fairly clean is called effluent.

A croft farmer only has what is necessary.

The stuff that comes out of a volcano is malt and larva.

Philadelphia means 'the City of Brotherly Love'.

What will Britain be free of in the 1990s?
Industry, sir?

Less people are born in developed countries therefore the population has slowed down.

The peopul in developing countries are eliterit.

The place of the film where mountains took part in *The Sound of Music* was Austria.

Warsaw is the capital of Pololand.

What is the significance of the continental shelf?
It provides good breeding-grounds for the fishermen.

Examples of root crops are turnips, swedes and marigolds.

At the geography lesson the teacher asked the class to look at their knives when they went home to see where they were made (expecting Sheffield). Next day one little boy put up his hand and said his knives came from Ferranti.

Eskimoes live in Iceland and rub noses as a greeting probably to keep warm. It is the only part of their body not covered up as they have to breathe.

The Venetians go about in Gladiolas.

Translations of a Kind

Language teachers are used to correcting errors but some of them are redeemed by their unconscious humour:

Exegi monimentum aire perennius. I have eaten a mountain harder than brass.

Maecenas atavis edite regibus. His grandfather ate kings for supper.

In Platonis libris omnibus fere Socrates exprimitur. Socrates was nearly squeezed out of the omnibus by Plato's children.

Genae puellae formosae sunt. Beautiful girls are cheeky.

Urit me Glycerae nitor. I am being burned by nitroglycerine.

Fulminantis magna manus Iovis. The thundering big hand of Jove.

Talia cum agentum mors praeventit. Death overtook him and he returned to Italy.

Very well, my son. *Très puits, mon soleil.*

Ça va bien? Are you going as well?

La Propriété c'est le Vol. Private Ownership is Theft.

L'Anglais avec son sang-froid habituel. The Englishman had his usual bloody cold.

Est-il parti, ma tante? Is there a party? My aunt.

La raison du plus fort est toujours la meilleure. The biggest raisins are the best.

Prenez garde que votre cheval ne prenne pas le mors entre les dents. Take care that your horse doesn't die of toothache.

Elle me conta son cas. She counted me her cash.

La pauvre femme turna vers . . . The poor woman turned green.

J'ai hâté de l'embrasser. I hated to embrace her.

Je frappe, la sentinelle ouvre. I knocked the sentinel over.

L'encre est sèche. The uncle is dry.

Un Espagnol de forte taille. A spaniel with forty tails.

Il m'a tant frappé. He struck my aunt.

Un grand garçon à lunettes. A big lunatic boy.

54

Il avait un couteau à la main. He made a curtsy to the sink.

L'usine était située dans un quartier désert. A quarter of the factory was deserted.

J'ai grand faim. I have a big wife.

Dieu et mon droit. My God your right!

Le garçon avait trois ans. The boy had three asses.

Joie de vivre. Whisky.

Tout à fait. He had everything made.

Emporté par la colère. Carried off by the collar.

Honi soit qui mal y pense. He may be honest who thinks badly.

Tatez cette étoffe: elle est mince. Taste this stuff, it's mince.

Le grand-pére – the piano.

La bougie – the mouth you speak through.

Présence d'esprit – a dead person.

Le chef de gare – the chief cook.

Au bord de la mer – all aboard the train.

One of the famous sights in Paris is the Sacre Coeur (The Sacred Cow).

Beurre – cold.

Les Peupliers minces frissonnaient dans la forêt.
The people were frying mince in the forest.

Through the Microscope

Respiration is caused by wearing a heavy sweater on a hot day.

Plants are different from animals because they do not go to the toilet.

A membrane is a brain with a very long memory.

The light passes through the lens and is focused on the rectum.

Yeast is the protection inside a cow around its liver.

Osmosis is a fertiliser you put round flowers.

To treat a patient for shock, rape him in a warm blanket.

Monkeys eat bananas as well as human beings.

The alimentary canal runs from your mouth to the rectory.

Comatose – dead feet, like when you get frostbite.

Snails have to slide along and hope for the best.

An octopus is a flat sort of fish with eight testacles.

Hair is sort of threads coming out of your head; they grow just like they was living.

Get a peanut, weigh it, burn it to nothing and then reweigh it.

The spine is a bunch of bones that runs up and down the back and holds the ribs together. The skull sits at one end and I sit at the other.

Pins and Pancakes

Interfacing is to stop your arms and neck fraying.

Before you can make a dress you must have a pattern, or if you are very experienced you can cut it out of your head.

Rhubarb is a kind of celery gone bloodshot.

Old people often eat a lot of cheap carbohydrate and can become stricken with illness or obscenity.

A common disease of cereal crops is wheat germ.

A sherrif is a French cook.

Written in one girl's exercise book in the cookery class was the following recipe:

Apple Crumble:

3 oz margarine	1lb apples
4 oz plain flour	2oz sugar

Method: Slice ruhbarb . . . sprinkle sugar over ruhbarb
Place breadcrumbs on top of ruhbarb.

(From a Home Economics note book) 'To clean a room, cover up the furniture with sheets, sprinkle the carpet with tea leaves, carefully sweep the room into a dustpan and throw it out of the window.

Keeping in Tune

Rumpelstiltskin was a Nationalist Composer from Russia.

Mozart lived until the end of his life.

. . . the famous Russian composer Ripsikcornetoff.

An aria is a very slow, laxative piece of music.

Q. What is this note called? ○
A. A semi-beaver.

After Wagner's death there was a Festival held every year in Bayreuth in his horror.

There are three sections in an orchestra – string, brass and woodworm.

Mozart died from salvation.

Two crotchets make a quaker.

Violin strings are made from cat's whiskers.

Pizzicato means to puke.

One of the smallest members of the percussion family is the tangerine.

Q. Where are the Proms held?
A. In the left hand.

Q. Why is the town of Bayreuth important in the world of music?
A. Because Mozart was killed there in a car accident.

A scale is an exercise for loosening the fingers. There are two types, diatonic and teutonic.

An Inspector Calls

'An inspector came to our school today. At first we thought he was the new janitor, but he asked questions that a janitor wouldn't ask.'

An inspector took a teacher to task for telling her pupils the meaning of words without leading them to discover it for themselves. To illustrate the point he took the lesson and came to the word 'prancing', which nobody knew the meaning of, so he began to walk around the room in a spirited way. 'Now, what am I doing class?' 'Please sir,' came the reply, 'walking in front of the teacher without saying "Excuse me".'

The inspector obtained the response that 'a pilgrim is a man who goes from place to place.' 'But I go from place to place. Am I a pilgrim?' the gentleman asked. 'No no, sir, a pilgrim's a good man.'

After an inspection of a small school the inspector noticed that a boy was busy drawing and when he asked him to let him see it the boy was reluctant, because he had drawn the gentleman. When the teacher went to fetch it, the little lad whispered, 'Please miss, I've put a tail on him and made it into a wee dog.'

A headmaster was irritated by members of the public entering the playground and using the school toilets. He instructed the janitor to lock the door on the next person he saw sneaking in. Within the hour the janitor managed this and handed the headmaster the key. After an hour or so the headmaster unlocked the toilet and released an infuriated Inspector of Schools.

Afterflaws

My mother wasn't healthy and she was warned not to have children by her doctor.

He suddenly realized he needed her as he knew nothing about household choirs.

My arm was in a lot of pain so I told a nurse and she passed it on to a doctor.

Very slowly I began to make a rapid recovery.

They was very pleased and I said I would treat them to a slap-up meal including my beautiful dog and my best companion Ben.

My sister and her boyfriend canoed all evening on the front room sofa and I wasn't allowed in to watch television.

I think hanging should be brought back, gelatine, the lot.

The best part of the show was the great Alfredo and his performing loins.

On our trip to York we were allowed to see parts of the minister not normally exhibited to the general public.

Dear Sir, please excuse James from being late as I slept in the smorning.

Sarah knew she was being a bit erotic, but she had a reputation for having a very imaginative imagination.

The expression 'the pain got right into the rib' is unusual as it does not state where the 'rib' is, but the reader can guess. I think he uses it as he knows the reader will have a good idea of where and what it is.

A sixty-foot tree can break wind for up to 200 yards.

Q: Name two fillings for a duvet.
A: Jam and Cream.

He sighed a heave of relief.

The purpose of the black cloth over the belljar is to stop the plant from being distracted.

During the Napoleonic Wars crowned heads were trembling in their shoes.

Jesus was crucified and recycled on the third day.

Hamlet was the town where the rats invaded.

Why do I always get the blame? It wasn't me! Why do you always make me the skateboard?

I was passing water over a bridge, when suddenly I noticed the sleepy village in the distance.

Macbeth has altered the system of the higher archie.

Watership Down describes all the habits of the rabbits from their eating to their exscremating.

'Muttonchop whiskers' are those wee bits of hair that you get on chops from the butchers.

She was good at everything she done in school. She won the duck's award for three years.

A refugee keeps order at a football match.

Mushrooms always grow in damp places so they look like umbrellas.

If a lady should faint in church put her head between the legs of the nearest medical man.

A grass widow is the wife of a dead vegetarian.

What is a herbaceous border? One who boards all week and goes home on Saturdays and Sundays.

The jockey lost two of his teeth when the horse fell and had to be destroyed.

Dust is mud with the juice squeezed out.

Snoring is letting off sleep.

A hostage is a lady who entertains visitors.

Tarzan is a short name for the American flag. Its full name is Tarzan Stripes.

Henry VIII had the Prayer Book put into English to spite the Pope, who wanted to marry Catherine of Arragon.

Prince Henry was drowned in the wash. The story goes that he never smiled again.

At the Battle of Crecy the English moved down the French with their hoes and barrows.

Henry had an abbess on his knee, which made walking difficult.

The Battle of Sluys was fought at sea. It was one of those battles in which the bowmen did better work than the cavalry.

It is dangerous to walk there at nights. I might be murdered and have to go without my tea.